SIREN OF ATLANTIS

SIREN OF

CEDAR SIGO

ATLANTIS

WAVE BOOKS SEATTLE & NEW YORK

Published by Wave Books
www.wavepoetry.com

Wave Books titles are distributed to the trade by
Consortium Book Sales and Distribution
Phone: 800-283-3572 / SAN 631-760X
Library of Congress Cataloging-in-Publication Data
Names: Sigo, Cedar, author.
Title: Siren of Atlantis / Cedar Sigo.
Other titles: Siren of Atlantis (Compilation)
Description: First edition. | Seattle : Wave Books, 2025.
Identifiers: LCCN 2024038699 | ISBN 9798891060135 (paperback)
Subjects: LCGFT: Poetry.
Classification: LCC PS3619.I473 S57 2025 | DDC 811/.6—dc23/eng/20240823
LC record available at https://lccn.loc.gov/2024038699
The Lovers tarot card on page vi by Salvador Dalí first published in 1984.
Designed by Crisis
Printed in the United States of America
9 8 7 6 5 4 3 2 1
First Edition
Wave Books 122

ז
LOS
ENAMORADOS
VI
VI
THE LOVERS
♏

I stood
indifferent to the rasp of metal,
and her eyes met mine;

you say, I could not see her eyes
across the field of battle,
I could not see their light

shimmering as light on the changeable sea?
all things would change but never
the glance she exchanged with me.

—H. D., *Helen in Egypt*, "Pallinode" 4.3

SIREN OF

ATLANTIS

RAYOGRAPH

Tangible reflection
of the fissure
leaning at rest
against the wall

a Polaroid
treatment of despairing
poets
dissolving into
flecks
of sunlight

hands on knees
on steps

several ambient movements
finally embossed

both hands on head
shown two ways
out of the tomb

the hillside windows
fogged and stuck open

a sanded figure kneels
no eyes
the sun at its
most ruthless
torn edge

the bamboo flooded
and became a bridge
in a few stained
brushstrokes

hang the image
off a string of others

last rays
overexposed
now frozen
to the garden
grass

two black birds
pinpointed
and broken apart

the death of one
is many

TEXTING SPELL

Wash and dry
my hands
obscure our central
point of contact
his necklace
and small talk
in the mirror
oblong inedible
cubes

Each word
being worth less
than its
equivalent note
the embargo
on content
felt fine
and I remain
unbothered
I coast routinely
upon the remains
of pure music
a few lanterns

get lost
in the dust up

The rain is a
wobbling
harp
a snake
in the frosted
grass
a black gleam
to the pipe
wax castings
of threads

The sauna is nearly
empty (echoing)
it must be ripped
from its bedrock
bisected
and filmed
bone white
lips pursed
door shut

The overflowing
fountain at night
desperate
western formations
perfume
on charcoal

glossy
almost
without design

Shaving foam
left
on a mirror
pulled from
Lascaux
spotted
and somewhat
soft

Planetary orange
and yellow vowels
at the tip
of my finger
the roof of my mouth

A vomitorium
is lost
without its close-up
a man of alabaster
draped in
black
and fit
Where is the palace
iodine?
I had misremembered
his hand

as being blurred
in motion
his single eye
kitchen table
early morning
sunlight

Lay my figures bare
                              and give them no rest,

I can relate to his premise, that he was born on Saturn

and must be getting back soon,

that the earth is a failed planet,

that rehearsal itself
                              becomes a ceremony.

STRANGER (FULL TEXT) #2

I toss my stencils
to the neon fire and begin to build,
stacking obsidian dust,

a text that betrays the shape of a tone,
a semblance of pitch,
the opposite of rubbing down
onto a headstone.

The mirage of white dawn on treated black,
wavering then solid states,

hovering over the exact spot
where the sun
strikes a songbook in tablets.
Wandering the edge of a crypt of lines and
having to carry them all back (still unseen).

Before every reading I was asked to quietly
rebuild the field of composition (wood and thin wire)
but always in a public corner
the audience was allowed that tiny bit of footing

before demanding my disappearance,

restricted to the few syllables that I could float
through the door.

More of a crook in the mouth,
the sweep of the tongue that floods the canal,

the water was a single cursive crossed-out line.

Keeping language lit and locked up,
bronzed or betraying its wear pattern,
a galaxy spiked with mist,
cold tintype
clouded red with black.

I fashion the gate
toward one arm of dystopia,
the concrete index
sold off as bits of poetry.

A system bent on interpretive orchestration,
the stacking and rubble of debris,
then scoring its outline.

All slivers angle toward the beloved,
sparking the end
of the tip of the night,

the light never quite settles.

STAR JASMINE

FOR BERNADETTE MAYER

Did you know there is still a bathhouse in Troy?
A handful of the guys swim over from Albany apparently.
Have you had any real long-term trouble sleeping?
"On Sleep" from *Indigo Bunting* is a masterpiece
of unflinching clinical precision and humor.

Are there specific things that happen in a poem
that can prevent it from becoming a sonnet?
Besides *Stanzas in Meditation*, which is your all-time favorite
work by Gertrude Stein? Mine is *Ida*.
Grand outings and shopping and small dogs in concentric circles,
another valentine inscribed in secret.

Did you ever return to Lenox after the period detailed in *Piece of Cake*?
How many *Utopias* remain in your closet?

*

Drowsily sitting around half watching,

she tried working more desperately despite the synesthesia

The light in the cave grew yellow and began to move about uneasily

There was a flash and rumble of thunder which were heard from this inner room

The other poets were on their feet gathered together in the corner

They frequently consulted one another and from the opening of the cave could

hear the guard stationed there.

⋆

It was her willingness to transcribe
throughout a condemned hall of mirrors,
clutching the camera.

"We will organize readings in the street,
screenings . . .
Christmas on Earth!"

Ed's shadow filmed as a spider
unleashed in a swing,
rather tired xylophone,
frantic strings,
bats and pangolins,
entwined scarab.
The odd rainbow skinned
throughout history,
left wobbling in carbonite,
particle boards
rotted out, glistening

restorative liquid. Five
page dreams left open,
then the requisite field
never blank.

Morning fed on the light
against aluminum rooftops,
very many layered.

*

Tending to the red thread

thrown within the garden.

She tracks its estrangement and

cooks down the spoils,

clips innocent roses from the tiny

bronzed bush. A lava like fountain

has lost its head and the registration

of the frame warps. Her tones

enraged dissonance—

factoids deflation.

The polar star

with gold leaf backing,

blinding sensational crowds.

*

The delicate cranes shall drink from the milk of black nylon
as they refuse to drink the scotch,

a ghost of star jasmine
loose in the basement night

embroidered with pearls

and feeling outmaneuvered I stood up Nathaniel Hawthorne
over the simple fact
of sleeplessness.

I left Melville dangling over an expanse of cold gray ribbon,
imperceptible breeze
blowing him back.

It was later a filthy dream like seascape
left to rot upon a wall
of solid build-up,

a narrow branch of bar room lights.

Orange trees were crowding the midnight
sands till Corfu,

blue city of the oranges.

A woman was climbing due east into my backyard of blank stars

(the language).

SAINT OF THE ABYSS

Well I myself am not myself —Joanne Kyger

Third day home:

We anchor our boat beside the most terrific strains of music

As the sky goes dark, I am overwhelmed by romance

"I just go to pieces . . .
. . . you're my thrill"

the paper folds
in one corner

then takes
on the light
straight through

Clouds stand in rings over the treetops

The canal continues moving
                                        in dotted lines

The moon sits low and crowds us (even outside)

*

I think I had my stroke
just to get out of reading for free

with million-dollar paintings on the walls

⋆

My favorite work of art
an eagle feather
fallen from the sky

complete with the first
gesture
to bend and lift it
off the ground

bead then hang it
upside down

⋆

Poetic gestures of internment or straight up tagging onto the walls,
under non reflective glass in frames, in font,
words carved in reverse through the screen
with hauntingly long trains of gowns
and the blood tapered through the underbrush
our installation to hint at its continuous river stepping in-and-out
is an event a storyboarded comic we want
recreated as ephemeral but still printed (names) more internment
language tossed onto the page as a weapon asleep

that was simply one afternoon spent bent down
scribbling entirely focused and entwined with space
I am allowed to run a little ahead of myself or not?
The idiots' secret, what is it like to write well?

⋆

Ode to The Hi-way House

OK calm down, let's also say
there is no need to write anything down for a while.
Let's think back on all the poets that may have flirted in this room
or fucked or tried to or met often, in semi secrecy several times a week.
For now, I feel silenced by the everyday I already told you,
diseased and purposely kept from new love and old.
And then Margaret dreamt that she and Barbara
drove back-up through the desert 900 miles
to leave cooked food in front of room 217. I call Lydia to say that Kazim
is teaching a whole Naropa summer course on Yoko Ono.
I hope this means a retelling of the Chambers Street
concert series with Jackson Mac Low.
This constructed attempt at poverty so chic I can forgive.
Especially if real poets were there as specimens taking part.
Any other poets that may have collapsed halfway down the hallway
of the archive? The ones that barely made it.
They make the rest of us smell so sweet; it becomes unreal.

1

The war has gone fully internal at the moment—green snot—night sweats—I set a lock out on my creaking door.

2

Yesterday, I was being paid to fight off the assertion that Native thought and philosophy could lie down next to the bride of white theology. It didn't work the first time around and now we have so-called allies crowding the entrance, an almost separate crusade.

3

"Lucidity is the wound closest to the sun"—from René Char's war journal, *Leaves of Hypnos*. I think of Beckett and the last line in his translation of Apollinaire's "Zone," "Sun corseless head," or Roger Shattuck's take on the same line: "The sun a severed neck."

4

Money is a war of the unknown future, forcing yourself to say "yes" out of fear that no other work will come. I now know that the poem, in all of its parts, will come forward to embrace the future.

5

Last night I decided to write my way out the door. I finally picked up on Lewis Warsh's tone of voice, it was such a heavy almost paranoid tone that it is still being filtered right now, like river water.

*

(1980s Reservation Sonnet after Wanda Coleman)

You are treated as a guest, we have drawn rings
that determine where you should remain (meaning your whole life).
We will pay for your health care and build spacious ghettos
of entirely separate houses, eerily painted in watercolor; ours was a soft chocolate brown.
After Mom left, she sometimes called while on the road or sent postcards.
I remember rereading one all day in my bed with no second sheet.
The Muppet Show in front of an orange velvet curtain.
My sister Lydia would nod in response to Mom's
questions from the road. "Are you being good?"
The phone was indeed heavier then.

The washer or dryer was always broken
and I knew enough not to ask which.
I remember commodities and recipes that died in vain.
How to bleach out the taste of a metal can.

⋆

(Fragment—after Coolidge)

There are no floors and there is no coast
There is no when
a cul-de-sac from which the stone still lives entirely covered with snow
cafe on the sodden marble enclosed in dreams,
Message from crystal lace:
"The sparrow is in the shale wheel."
A wall of yellow plates before the urge nearing solution,
the shine on garnet
the cuff marks of speech
One crust, my limitless variable pitch
It's easy to pretend that it's beginning again,
you learn to love the toggle and the witness, the ash staved into a wall.

⋆

Back home from the hospital
The cat avoids me

I am a ghost
of my former self

⋆

"And the uniformity relates happily only to the mechanical process"

"Merchants under wrote the hazards of export caravans and voyages"

⋆

The carousing red middle of the kerosene lamp, the cat inches off the record player. I can hear a few nightbirds through the screen, upstairs. I walk the hall and whisper John Wieners's lines from *707 Scott Street*, those that failed me this morning, "*For I have looked down into the pit and turned away trembling.*"

⋆

You die and fall through space
                    to lie as an outline

memory is a few shattered pieces lost

        no lilies on earth were ever mine,
        plucked from a spring, in secret

A rush of figures
spring out from middle hell,
                        the darkened

faces that linger in back
                                        wandering

Completed August 13, 2022

I suffered a stroke in late July of 2022. As I was reentering my body, I decided to try writing poetry again. (I was still endlessly flipping fragments in my head and reorganizing them.) The following poems seemed to come out as a series of exhibits, a naïve garden that I forced myself to connect into something larger. It is a gift to be reintroduced to your practice. I seem to be happy to cling to these poems without stamping them good or bad as they were rightly or wrongly all I had going at the moment, like writing a textbook or a portfolio that fills up almost accidentally. "The Vertical Room" is the last example of the series published here. I suspect that in some way I will always be learning to write again—"keeping my hand in," as a friend once put it.

When I am Earth
I stand perfectly still
at a slight angle

When I am Water
I vanish quickly into crevices

When I am Fire
I brandish heat among
clusters of frozen starlight

When I am Wind
I string loose figures
onto a clothesline
and lean back
hands up in surrender

HOUSE-SITTING

I had been
talking back
to the cat's meow
from behind
a painted door.

"Hello Sweetheart"
"It's O.K."
"You are such a sweet . . ."

I had been
talking
to the cat,

and not
the lovesick
person

I could
not see

standing
beside it
in the dark.

MEMORIZATION SONNET

The common vernacular is our movement
and should never be reduced to echoes of voice.
We should not prize that which is withheld,
like the ever shifting, beckoning
book of devotional letters, “all departures”
as some master poet once said quoting Cecil Taylor.
The room is several books deep
at this point you can tip it, fluid, in reverse.
The west end of the apartment is coated in frost.
While they drone on about positions
you should be assuming new ones,
zoned out with your notebook
(a line that bends upward to express *alarm*).
Maintain this cranial document that runs alongside your life
(somewhat successfully)
“A stately pleasure dome
smoking, drinking, nonchalance”
or was it some pressing quote from the Confucian Odes
overheard at a doomed rent party?
Atmosphere later set in stone, and you could sell it off
as a rowhouse framed in candlelight, trim and gavel.
Trampled wrapping paper waves
left lapping beneath the floorboard.
It was early morning when I fell back to sleep.

HÔTEL FRANÇOIS

I think very well of Donald trimming his trees and scaring off the deer.
I think very well of Jackie hosting and dealing in pictures.
I think very well of John making the most mischief and each night crowded with the
possibility of poetry.
I think well of Ellis and his insistence on more screen time, addicted to "unboxing"
videos.
I think well of Anselm, that he drags his loose and gleaming fender back and forth to
an unfixed, agitated measure.

⋆

Why do they get forgotten when we run so desperately off the fumes of youth?
Everything is inherited only as indefinable, as a bronzed Jean Arp with sullen gut.
The satin endings can be reattached or sent out with an assistant to become soapstone.
I want the most satanic podium for others to decipher, line upon line.
Liquid Crystals and *The Emerald Tablet*, incredibly heavy titles, think "mausoleum."
Several points flowing together in stonework.
Off-white, always a pleasure to remember, have a bad habit.

⋆

This could be, it has its possibilities, the moon and stars rounded up in a cold sky. I walked up to my room alone or so I thought until you kissed me, blessing my subsequent body. I was shocked but went along with some enjoyment assuming that I would uncover more later. I had to fly back to the West Coast early the next morning, which made this episode feel extremely lyrical, like a song you can't get out of your head, so hearing the song in real life feels unnecessary. We won't look back upon the once colossal promise of an interview between us, our feelings have made language seem slow to catch up. I only use words like stones because you are far away, and I want to believe that they connect us across the stars.

II

This cloud of souls has wandered all over the sky,
gone to the corner store and may never come back
I have dreamed of your face for three nights and each time
it rises, it redefines itself
You warn of general dangers and rise quickly to leave
iced over fears, born of an iron ship torn in half
and the silhouette in aggregate placed in a tiny doorway,
his expression a touch bewildered
The city is run by enterprising zombies and occasional artists
I choose to sit in the center of an empty white room as a half dead flower
The net of dream and interdependence gets torn throughout the night
—haphazard curses begin to fly (one thousand years of infamy)
What good is all of this when I am left for dead and looking on?

The same method of successive layers of building, they had conquered ignorance through leering at each other. In my mind it seemed empty artifices continually kept on at the virtues of poverty, walking in the woods of each individual century with crystals, shells and engravings tossed aside. I waited some time to fake the excavations of old cities and make it into a game, idling on the lake left alone in the vast hall where a carriage came in noisily as though a character in a book. Weakness in my chest dark brown table at the foot of something I could not see. Colored hairs jut over empty space where words (clearly threatened) began to draw their costumes. The trick of leaving light as fluid in a field. Shipbuilding and navigational robes become known redemptive cloth (combed out) and I lock the maps away that indicate the advancing wave of young angels, they were fine with seeing someone after being dead awhile. Before today projecting myself into place all at once. A terrace laid out as a round garden walking about and playing with brushes, energy which then layers, peddling filth and a great number. Moments pass to extinguish brilliant prisms. Some black slabs with silver spots appear farther on. I will write some leaf shadows that hang along the wall dreamlike. Grey or brown, boiling in front of my eyes.

Details I can remember as far
as being a writer . . .

and the Spanish
stationed in
          different locations,

a repeating gun

               quite early in the afternoon.

The sky is streaked with

                    any number of barrels full.

                    First,
there is some basic improv   some dream
reversing itself outward
like Hans bent over the man scribbling enormous smiles,
one of Miriam Hopkins' guns

     that shoots large holes at the back of my neck.

Breaking through scraps

of a drafting table,
such was that vision
or a quick absorption

of basic exploding weapons. The silvered bathing bowls

could sink a galleon.

The greatest sadness:

ideas similar to mine, sea routes of mine,

I am led quite a distance,

where still shown the last fumes, the crystal cut fruit.

THE ART OF MAKING DANCES

FOR SARAH ENID HAGEY

The fire is courted openly \ strings driving the bark of hounds

Gold is thrown in handfuls down the staircase \ a tremor in bed

The crystal bookends sit higher than my head \ giant, crowned in shadow

Every arrangement still cut for tension \ the bishop is yanked along

Robe trailing an awful angle / all that is allowed onstage

In tiger eye or cagey red wig / melted marble with green jacks

Very studied basic movements that provoke silence and humor

Carried over in exquisite type and tone of voice / the timing out of line

The reach in her voice / across continents

Drama plus decay / wobbling billion-dollar intonations

SAND

His footing is light itself. A slim shepherd of wolves, his teeth are momentary lights that sting our eyes, excursions. His death rattle shapes the forest floor. A sudden hand splits timbers of oak. You are a worn-out film playing in my heart. When it is finally dark, the enchanted bodies begin to slip from between the cypress. I swell, bored with the same longing; the sun emerges as a short square. Shadows tilt, you linger just out of reach. A fountain gurgles in the square, lulling me to sleep. Our mornings are still secret, you greet my soul sending a rested wave. I could never turn outright cold, swathes of blood at night obscure my vision. Our boredom is a daughter of indiscretion, memory pleads at the same bronze gate. Trim down these clouds of dust, the air is still from now on. My eyes turn clear and mirrored at the foot of the spring.

After G. Ungaretti

A SCANDAL IN PERIL

Clear light and illusion become one
these murals are "for" not "of" the dead.
Two stone heads, sunken garden adorned
in weak calypso breezes plural
shadowed in carpets, hung as one dome.
No immediate reflection nor surface
tension interwoven. The yantra is in free float
inversion. The sun is a wide
stone circle, flat gray.
The approach to music is still stanzas,
a register I no longer have to fight for exactly,
I have lived here indefinitely.
A wet handful of old ballads, scattered ash, and lime,
badly smeared nothingish dahlias,
dry stems cross, tugging at the bright knit of the metal.
What amounts to the blind wrap around
hustle of the paint, one crooked and ongoing
unapologetic gesture.
It's the neon white that lightens the boxcar,
a truly heavenly rise from pavements field theory.
What a relief his work is without those
flaunted figures anymore, I mean
faces destroy me, those hacked out from the legend
now here in reverse relief, standing back.

We don’t need middle henchmen, period,
nor to drive to the office every morning anymore.
I refuse a plagiarized request to recuse myself.
Through mountains of tape
and beautifully redacted death poems
a scandal in peril emerges.
The samsara of fuckedupedness
has caused the hall mirror to split
and a nearby stupa to foreclose
now facing the red sky.
I blame the new poetic forensics,
orange flower and rose are more like flavors
than a solid light we live inside of
or bend to our fleeting will,
no moat linking paradise
and there is hardly one posture to align with this.

It was a dick ghost genocide
It was a beastie boy's hotness I hadn't seen before
It was a full-on panic, a rooftop escape in the dead of night
It was a not-so-secret morning kiss on the rooftop
It was a romantic ghost story of old New York
with the streets full of carts and stalls and hooks catching
It was a match book posing as a book of poetry
the opening page was blank and bright baby blue
It was a songbook worth billions but stuck in three changes
It was a book of prophecies braided with random clerical work, lists and abandoned bits
of memoir, Solitary Pleasure.

HISTORICAL MELODRAMA

Lock me away again
beneath a staircase
where I continue to sing
the part of Orpheus,
                    rewritten, without lyre.

"Sleep escapes me still."

Everyone in the half-empty
playhouse can hear it,
now struggling
                    to hear every sound,
looking behind one another
and angrily
over their shoulders.

A SPIRAL AND A STAR

Driftwood (bright white) turns the flame
blue at its base,

Diane's slight shake and
dry mouth

I watched her turn young again
and then a bit drawn and whimsical
as we became reacquainted.

Put to work at her bedside
transcribing tiny new Revolutionary Letters, Dawn Poems,
snares that are set to explode across centuries

into further collapse?

Dream after Christchurch

after Freddie Mercury writhing up against your ear

turn heretic
and teach me the changes, elated
deep in dream
where I might find you
turning again, slender to the night.

-In memory of Diane di Prima-

RELIQUARY

FOR JOHN BOSWORTH

It was the flutter of ultimate arrangement
betrayed in a nervous hand.

The upper limit skies,
their peeling apart,

we must afford ourselves the nude body
if nothing else.

I mismatched edges and admired when I couldn't.
I heard a knot of wood, a snap as in the arc of a stove fire

left asleep in the back
seat steel of a Plymouth

let the stars off early
soon as I
get them flicked
back on

we trampled the late fall
as through a snake pit

staircase left
to waver

the grille marks
faint

fields of white rock
held loose
at the heels of dusk

The first time they reappear
we've forgotten all about them.
                    Treacherous mornings
take on the weight
of missteps (in series?)

canned explosions
set off the most awkward age.
A county square now tilted
uncrossed, awash with daydreams.

A rondelle served in kind
as a slap can be.
The spike of a line driven
across
into battle.

A flag of grand mishearing.
Jupiter bright
rushes left,

a black sky is kept warm
strangled of its few stars
sewn on red,
ochre, yellow and white.

DIRECTIONAL FIELD WITH COLUMNS

All trees
are trees
of knowledge
depending on
where they hang
momentarily
upon
a light
system.

⋆

How does the wardrobe change within the scheme of a paragraph? Does poetry ever wish to ride a line of prose in hopes of revealing more? Do we wish to be dissonant yet confined to a room of four corners? Is it an assignment we give ourselves to check the quality of images? They leap from my mind when doubled over. Thankfully the prose poem has been used to countless (warring) formal ends and so remains a pulsating phantom container.

⋆

That's the problem with doors
they force my hand
and never swing broadly enough
for the lazy second half of my mind.

The details that I keep encoded,
they get rearranged but never spoken about thoroughly.
Vocalization is over, highly wrought opinions get shot down.
Let them topple over
until they recognize my silhouette among the ruins.
Occasional tulips and blown-out confetti, industrial songs,
let the body coil gently along the empty shore.

⋆

"I still don't know what a prose poem is, but it creates worlds."

The roots
            wet with permission
                                    form a staggered crown.

"Just write what's going on around you, outside and inside."

"It's a conceptual universe that involves a certain number of words."

How they jostle for three seconds on the degraded lava. It's a faded, star reliant system almost washed away by mass adoration. The doubled screens absorb a lot of astral blowback. It's a voice cutting in from the side and finding its measure in spillage. How do I accidentally make clear my otherworldly derangements, they may prove useful, widening the trail with red, reflective tile. A series of fountains lie in state, whistling bottle rockets disregard their own report.

December 4, 2023

THE LAST NIGHTS

At the door he suggested that I look in through the window. For several days the rain continued to fall. Paris covered itself in a veil. He seemed to be addressing his remarks to an orange couch, but his gestures made it clear that he followed a secret voice of diversion, one of those poets chosen through chance. There were months during which he lived under one certain sign (that of being followed). I didn't know him yet and that nothing bothered him. After my conversation with the most wasted of assassins it was easy to breathe in the alcohol of the open air. A lush garden drawn through the light of a man's eyes. I had no fear of forgetting. I dreaded the oncoming boredom of the unknown. Night succeeding daylight, digging its own pit. I was determined not to lose track of this phantom, more than anything else I hid from him under a river of quiet, under a cloud of time lost. I answered his smile without thinking, as one might answer the mirror.

The crumpled steel
guarded movement

its offering, dead
bells on felt
squares

walk your
body around its
outline, in some
distress and rust

you got it right

*

see through—
enter off
the sides

no edge left
unturned, blurred

in point of fact

a soft glow beckons
before we are barred

from the lights
the way we like

*

any number of ways
to squeeze a brushed
defenseless box

meaning mind pouring
holes down through
the top reinforcing
its phantom

dust coated tongues
of grey green plants
open prairie

*

I would like it better
strolling each side alone

iron grips

the long and dark
long and bright

divided

I count
on the fringe,
the armored night,
the right shirt,
the reckless stain.
A drained look
from the barman.
I sense a shift
in the level white
of his eye. Grime
is a coat painted
in duress. Fearing
occasional thunder,
sloshing through
the bathwater
of a joyously
drunken voice,
its flailing soft
crust,
"Words without vision
are deprived of stability."

TETRACHORD SONNET

Bands of seafoam widen
as the big top empties out

green helium escapes
a thin rim of scaffolding

Parade through irregular
                    smashed tubing
opaque as rainwater
                    in streaks

low groan and swaying of the tower
stern heads of orchids
                              and passersby

"When I signal to the mirror,

fire with this hand
and fall through that door."

CHATTER IN THE WAITING ROOM

Pathetic wet leaf that clings to a portal door

*

Another year
another wish to speak poetry
at all the in between moments.
I do, and all while changing direction.

No one is lost
they seem to follow me down.
Pick trillium flowers,
flirt in several staggered lines,
and move back inside.

I need the everyday in flux,
the practice of outside
is also dependent on
hysterical momentary retreat.

A fleeing from the flowered wood.

*

Time is a reinforceable frame,
I stop to examine
the overall weight.

⋆

A stripped back stone house
at the end of a slick street.
Ten stick figures
with black umbrellas

step out, and slip instantly.

⋆

Has the ghazal been trafficked and malformed beyond immediate usefulness?
What about the word *ceremony*?
Or the haiku being reintroduced (wrongly) inside of every elementary school screen?

"A bunch of poems told me that they were self-taught this morning."

"And the sparrows had hard times in the air."

"One helen is enough, trust me"

They were a phantom that played upon a wall
for only seconds,
the open fire that tricks the eye.

⋆

Playing out love's last day in a hand-stitched blue suit.

⋆

Don't put the room back together before we say goodbye.

⋆

I never think to purposely stay in the house all day.
The air is allowed more action with an open window.
Run this back, "I like it better, no one knows"
the age of the grating in the bronze square.

Intonations building up and through
to rip the concrete like a seam.
Interrupted all the way through with a single rusted wire.
Invisible plunge onto a blade
laid down so far inside that they could not see.

I sense pattern, holes, and warm sunken rooms,
run your hand along and feel for tenses.
A progression, climb up to the roof
and patch in the weakest square of sky.

⋆

I can hear you fine from down the hall.

⋆

When he tips back
the dance floor wanes
buckles
then gathers back.

An unclear dream: Jesse Ed Davis casting about Pershing,
Hollywood, North Hollywood
inland, shiftless out of step
and lovesick.

He turns back,
the phone shoots halfway down the block.

⋆

You question the lightning rod stuck
as active carving knife and then my unapologetic
bedhead in blurry series
a neck that bends queerly.

All the darkness has been settled
except in their eyes.

⋆

Their features so graceful
and the light of their soul
bleeding from delicate forms.

I am led toward one stack then another,
down the narrow staircases
until the sky is streaked with rose
and loaded down with liquid.
It dries slowly and curls
something similar to musk.

*

Locked up in a recently vacated boathouse.
Considered and rested, hanging out deep west.

Influx now so bright and beckoning without need,
it's categorically awkward.

I don't know that I want to be that stone
within their understanding anymore.

Does the web of conjoined radiance
hold the object at any one point?

Is it not directed in the least by our request?

*

Referring to city / I awaken

I write this in order to sleep.

Falling back asleep

ruinous to the quick,

Saint Paul in genuine shock
facing the blue mirror
boring still life
same old aqueduct and fluted
evidence

the above adornments.

March 1–6, 2023

Maybe I just like the way the bass is mic'd and their filthy talk.

The sun is a stone upending its curve toward the edge.

Every frame should belong to the dancers
edging away in delight,
in separates, swept hair on a sunken ship.

I could always hear a cliff's edge staggered
in his day long piano works.

Only lines that could withstand repeated annunciation,

the off day recorded.

These patterns become light
strewn within
other crystal.

⋆

"Over railroad station tracks
faintly flickers"

what other circumstance
might we mesh
so my body
might jump to
slither and follow suit,
we run away,
the paint scuffing the paper
better than a breathing pattern
smeared lightly
but never ended
indented again

*

"Into numberless
reflections
rises a smile from your eyes"

Twist him off three rods of yellow gold,
sometimes red, sometimes rose.

He seems the best poet for constantly rethinking
his relation to weaponry,
for lodging the jewel in the eye of the camera.

"Just crack it open and walk away."

Without blueing or blackening,
without a metal rinse,

twist him off a Spanish helmet,
armored breastplate,

any and all silver
necessary
to protect his horse.

SIREN OF ATLANTIS

I've strayed too far off the block for mine own kind
and writing is not necessarily editing right now if it's the amusement of disguise
over disappearance. If it's become all about dressing well and getting back to
gallerists while still in my plucked helmet storming about. Is it a generative
loneliness? Like rebuilding my body within a passage of light? Is this the right
key for the empty apartment? Jay is reading Valery Larbaud in a tangle
of light at springtime. Which specific title escapes my vision but
the platinum tip of my tail is underwriting every emotive and syllabic outburst,
every instance of enraged punctuation and jealousy over not sleeping over
where there was no intended manger to begin with. Where I am to be aired out prior
to introduction. Privy to his incredible feats of disappearance carried off
in the alleyways of a Greenpoint night. I bow my staff upon a skinned knee.
Happy to be a so-called songwriter again, a little something coming in,
whisking it all up, draped in fat lines down a dark room. Slamming shut
the so-called atmosphere of music.

WAVING AMARYLLIS

FOR ZOE BREZSNY

Crenulations of wasted lines
hang down on a stamped out
fistful of cadmium clay.

A rush to smear in
from under her nails.
She spoke of characterization
how the figures turn all lovingly refracted,

their undertones
left banded and bluish,
"I forget the healing specificities of that crystal."

Some glorious passage within gets hammered out.

The two waves are washed as one, strung and hobbled over with neon light,

the one arch yellow
we can all agree on.

⋆

"Be green in the order of solids,
perceived as a cloud"
a window fogged over

not left open.
The bluest of pockets
soaked through

leaning on the mute,
clumsy slashes
at the armor

torn
corrugated
useless as cash.

There's nothing to
talk about
inside the glass

or the white box,
you were not allowed
to connect such darkness.

Many are lost
fragments of thought
barely held.

The bride was meant
to rest in the center
cube formation,

sane lines
of etching or
severed then repeated

heart bracing accidents?
Just unload then drape in Lucite
the bride has a center.

⋆

The rousing current of the water betrays its snow cold potential. A final circus dive just after they have turned their backs.

I'm still piecing a body back together. I think of its audience as one enormous side long glance.

Allowing for the square pool of a soundtrack to refill itself, the swept in smoke of a foxed page, a leak I could not choose to fake again. It was a long sign up prior to another broken field search, a few shattered opals filled with watermelon tile.

There was a hidden inscription just below the morning drone, sitting pretty. Spider's legs are honorific, placed in glassine envelopes, type floated dead along the bottom. A printed page of lost blots.

CLOSE-KNIT FLOWER SACK

Seedless golden tears,
ferns bound to flesh at off angles,
busted out rez towns,
hemming us in with a cloak of mosses.
The orchestration needs tufts of black shadow,
incidental notes to weigh it down, the blanket depicts a field and loon.
I said we once formed kingdoms at the foot of a vanishing stone.
What was it I said that they said?
"vividness is self-selecting"
several points flowing together in stonework.
I only use words like stones because we are far away.
We corrupt a landscape through the planting of foreign flowers.
Borders are so often theorized as division
wending along with a spot of sunlight,
"the bone-frame was made
for
no such shock knit within
terror,
yet the skeleton stood up to it."
They are not artifacts but fit to our hand,
our daily voice,
the short mouth line erased.
The marsh revels in its glitter
and occasional cranberry.

The subject is left purposely unstable,
we will not be robbed of continuum.
The shells fly out from the dress,
on strings, according
to demands left in the music.
Certain stories are told in full frog regalia,
the music is allowed its wet set of wings
and room to lie down.
Words arranged for prayer
are in fact geometric forms
or portraits of poets themselves,
uncovering the dictates of a graven line.
Orlando, are we even
allowing ourselves the present
moment anymore?
There are still two blankets that sit on either side.
Reimagining can take place at the root of time,
out of all necessity
we convert the elements
as a matter of course.

THE PURSUIT

We stomp in
as they all turn

We drop our bunch of
daisies
paper and string
onto the floor

The Lovers—
a double girded myth
at my rough sleeve

Where the usual
sets of
syntactic arrangement

await
a sleepless tambor

Thin and melodious
melodrama
but kept
without occlusion
a spiral
showing off passage

⋆

Seems like all my work
is commissioned now
like I'm being embalmed
or, John Wieners once writ,
"girdled in gold."

I become taxed
a bit more
at land's end,
forgetful.

A neglected gown
gone to scrap
through daylight's
sorted window.

The gold of doll's hair,
a pair of scratches
I had tried to sweep up.

Painting the flame eating
velvet retardant
back onto mountains of crowns,
a largely crooked offing.

The sun stands
pliant, we hung its canopy
silk over head
to steady the lens
during contact.

The darkening of the doorframe.
We hope to catch that,
the want that is present.

⋆

Follow me down
through the locks
to pick each lily as sharpened
the pinning of the sandpaper
hat to the ace

dreams replay
through the pick in a line
its armor
each to its own
internal breezeway.

His shadow hides one shoulder
cut out from the dark
handheld rasp
with sky sprung,
stars embarrassed.
I stumble onto a quiver.
There is no key.

September 26–30, 2023

ACKNOWLEDGMENTS

Some of these poems first appeared in: *As of Late*, *Bæst*, *Bombay Gin*, *The Brooklyn Review*, *Building*, *Changes Review*, *FIELDNOTES*, *Julebord*, *New Overland Review*, *The New York Times*, *Puerto Del Sol*, *The Shade Journal*, *Ursula*, and *You Are Here: Poetry in the Natural World*.

Some of these poems first appeared in a chapbook titled *Saint of the Abyss*, from Spiral Editions.

"Waving Amaryllis" was first published as a broadside for a group show titled *Landline* at Personal Space in Vallejo, California.

Both "Texting Spell" and "Star Jasmine" were included in shows at Off Paradise in New York City: *Good Clean Fun* and *Some Kind of Mind Thing*, respectively.

"A Spiral and a Star" was printed as a broadside by Julia Seko at Naropa University in 2021.